As Sisters, We Share Something Special

Sister,
this comes to you
filled with all the joy,
tears, memories, and love
we've created together
through the years.
You've been the best sister
and the most perfect friend
anyone could ever ask for.
Sister, I love you.

— *Edmund O'Neill*

As Sisters,
We Share
Something Special

A collection of poems
Edited by Susan Polis Schutz

Blue Mountain Press ®

Boulder, Colorado

Library of Congress Catalog Card Number: 89-90661
ISBN: 0-88396-278-0

ACKNOWLEDGMENTS appear on page 62.

Manufactured in the United States of America
First printing: March, 1989

Blue Mountain Press ®

P.O. Box 4549, Boulder, Colorado 80306

CONTENTS

As Sisters, We Share Something Special

Through the years,
we've gone through many
good and bad times together.
There have been things
*   that we've disagreed on*
and things that have brought us
*   so close together.*
There have been the silences
*   that sisters, no matter how close,*
*   must hear,*
and there has been the laughter
*   that only sisters share.*
But through the years,
*   I've always known that*
no one could ever replace you
*   and the love we share.*

— Ann Rudacille

Sisters Have a Special Way
of Growing Closer
Through the Years

Girls will be girls
and friends will be friends,
but when you think of
sisters being sisters,
you know exactly how close
the feelings can be.

Sisters have a special way
of growing closer as
the years go by,
and the feelings they have shared
are always a very important part
of their lives.

*And though sisters may disagree
at times,
they ultimately accept each other
for the way they are,
and they know that
what really matters is the love
they feel for one another.*

— *Deanna Beisser*

A Wish Just for You, Sister

*For all the times when you need
the sun to shine through
your cloudy skies . . .
I want it to be there for you.*

*For all the times when you need
someone to turn to . . .
I will always be there.*

*I wish for lots of things for you,
but mostly, I wish for your happiness
and for a dream or two to come true.*

— Chris Gallatin

Sister, These Are
My Wishes for You

May you find serenity and tranquility in a world you may not always understand. May the pain you have known and the conflict you have experienced give you the strength to walk through life facing each new situation with courage and optimism. Always know that there are those whose love and understanding will always be there, even when you feel most alone. May you discover enough goodness in others to believe in a world of peace. May a kind word, a reassuring touch, and a warm smile be yours every day of your life, and may you give these gifts as well as receive them. Remember the sunshine when the storm seems unending. Teach love to those who know hate, and let that love embrace you as you go into the world.

May the teachings of those you admire become part of you, so that you may call upon them. Remember, those whose lives you have touched and who have touched yours are always a part of you, even if the encounters were less than you would have wished. It is the content of the encounter that is more important than its form.

*May you not become too
concerned with material matters, but
instead place immeasurable value on the
goodness in your heart. Find time in
each day to see beauty and love in the
world around you. Realize that each
person has limitless abilities, but each
of us is different in our own way. What
you may feel you lack in one regard may
be more than compensated for in another.
What you feel you lack in the present may
become one of your strengths in the
future. May you see your future as one
filled with promise and possibility.
Learn to view everything as a worthwhile
experience. May you find enough inner
strength to determine your own worth by
yourself, and not be dependent on
another's judgment of your accomplishments.
May you always feel loved.*

— Sandra Sturtz Hauss

Sister . . .
This Is for You

The nicest thoughts
and the best memories
a person can ever have
*   are not easily forgotten.*

And some of the best remembrances
I will ever hold in my heart
are the ones that
have to do with you.

It's easy to get lost in thought,
thinking about how much we've shared,
and smiling to realize
*   how close we've always been.*

I want you to know
*   what a special, exceptional person*
*   you are to me.*
I will always think of you
*   as my dearest and closest friend.*

— Collin McCarty

For My Sister,
with All My Heart

*Now that we are older
and so many things in our lives
      have changed,
I realize how lucky we are
to have shared so many wonderful
      times together.
Being children together was easy;
becoming adults was a challenge.
Yet now I think of you
and feel so proud for you
and the accomplishments you have made
      in your life.
I know you are special to others,
      and you are always special to me.*

You are my sister,
and with all my heart,
  I hope that all your dreams
    for tomorrow will come true
and that love
will be with you forever.

— *Deanna Beisser*

Sister, would you like to know
what I would wish for you,
if I could have any wish I wanted?

If I could have any wish I wanted,
   this is my wish . . .

That in your life,
   which is so precious to me,
may troubles, worries, and problems
never linger;
may they only make you
that much stronger and able
and wise.

And may you rise each day with
sunlight in your heart,
success in your path,
answers to your prayers, and
that smile — that I love to see —
   always there . . . in your eyes.

— Carey Martin

A Message
for My Very Special Sister

I don't think I let you know
as often as I should,
but I'm awfully glad
that you're my sister . . .
*   and I often think of you*
*   and the very special love*
*   we share.*

One of the things
I value most in my life
is sharing the same family with you.
We share a certain closeness
that can only be ours —
and few things are
as important to me as that.

Thank you, my sister,
for staying close
and for keeping our relationship
the focal point it has always been
for both of us.
I love being comfortable enough
to share myself with you,
because you bring stability
to the things
I'm learning to become.

— Robin Bonham

Thanks, Sister,
for Being So Wonderful

If everyone were to take
   a special moment
to say thanks for the blessings
   that come to us in our lives,
we would find many people's hearts
   reaching out to many different things,
and speaking of the different thoughts
         that bring them joy.

As I take a special moment like this
   to think of what I cherish,
my thoughts immediately go to a certain
   very wonderful person.
It's someone I have known all my life.
   I dearly love her, and I feel so close
      to her, even when I miss her.

I so often think of one of the things
   that I am most grateful for.

And that . . . is having you for my sister.

— Alin Austin

Being My Sister Makes You Different from Any Friend I've Ever Had

The other day
    I was trying to figure out
why you are different from any friend
    I've ever had.
You listen with an intensity
    that reveals your deep love for me;
you ask those questions
    that trigger my deepest feelings,
        and I see — more than before —
things I would be afraid to face
    alone,
things I'm relieved to release
    with you there.

As my sister,
   you hug me with a warmth
      that absorbs all my hurt,
and your eyes reveal
   an understanding and empathy
      that goes beyond casual observation.
You care enough to take on the burden of
   being me for a moment,
   to carry part of my pain,
   to heighten all of my joy.
That's what makes you so different.

That's what makes you my sister.

— Denise Vega-Perkins

Sisters and Friends

Sometimes I wonder if
   you and I are sisters
   who turned out to be
   good friends,
or if we are friends
   who just happen to be sisters.

No matter how
   it was meant to be,
   I'm glad that you've been
   both a sister and a friend
   to me.

— Shelly Johnson

Sister, I Wish So Much that We Lived Closer to Each Other

You are so much more than just
a sister to me.
You have been my strength
through so many rough times,
and my shoulder for endless tears
I have shed.
You have been my sounding board
when I had a crazy idea
    I needed to express,
and my companion when I was
    in the mood to be silly.
I think about you so often,
and wish we didn't have to
live so far apart.
Although we keep in touch
    with each other,
it's just not the same as seeing you,
hugging you, and sharing with you.

I feel so lucky, though,
because the bond we have developed
cannot be broken by distance
or weakened by infrequent visits.
Even apart, we share so many
*   unspoken thoughts*
and are able to relive
precious moments together.
Whether near or far,
I love you always, my dear sister.

— *Chris Ardis*

Sister, I just
wanted you to know . . .

I haven't told you lately
how much you mean to me,
and it's not because
I haven't thought about you . . .
I think of you very often
with fond and loving thoughts.

I don't ever want
to take your presence in my life
for granted.
You are too important to me
to do that.

What I'm trying to say is
I love you very much . . .
and I just wanted you to know.

— Debbie Avery Pirus

It's so nice having you for my sister . . .

You're the best kind of sister —
the kind who listens when I need
   to talk;
who cares when there is no one else.
You've given me courage when I
   had none
and strength when I needed it.
You've given compassion and
   kindness at any time.
You've always been there —
ready to listen, understand and
   love me for who I am.
You are my best friend . . .
   and I love you.

— Gwenda Isaac Jennings

With Love, from
Sister to Sister

I remember when we
  were children —
there seemed
an unspoken need between us
that we both be happy.
The time we have together now
always finds me wanting more,
and I need the comfort of knowing that
you are always happy,
the reassurance of believing that
whatever touches your life will be
kind and good.
You have always been so special to me,
and I am so happy to be your sister,
forever loving you.

— Carol Maatta Oberg

Thanks, Sister, for the Times You've Shared with Me

I just want to say thanks . . .
for all the times you kept me company
when I was alone;
for all the times you had patience
when I was still finding myself;
for all the times you surprised me
when I was feeling low;
for all the times you understood
when I myself didn't seem to;
for all the times you made me laugh
when I was about to cry;
for all the times you listened
when I had something on my mind;
for all the times you shared with me
your most precious secrets;
for all the times you hugged me
when I needed someone near;
for all these times, and many more,
thanks for being you.

— *Jane Alice Fox*

Sister, the Love We Have
for Each Other
Will Always Be a Part of Us

*W*e've had our differences
over the years,
experiencing pangs of jealousy
and competing against each other
as sisters often do.
We've gone through periods
of arguing
and periods of silence,
trying so hard to convince ourselves
that we have little to share
with each other.
I think we both know, though,
that our love for each other
runs very deep.

Sister, the love we share
comes from sharing so many
childhood experiences together.
How can we forget all
  the laughter,
  the expressions of our dreams,
  the warmth,
  and the support?
Although I seldom admit it,
especially to you,
I want you to know that
I admire you very much,
and no matter how hard
I might try to hide it,
my love for you is stronger than ever.
I'm so glad I had you to grow up with,
and even happier that I have you now
to continue with me through
this journey of life.

— *Chris Ardis*

Sister, I want you to know
something special
about my feelings for you . . .

S*ister,*
sometimes I feel a need
to tell you
what a beautiful part
of my life you are.

And I just want you to know
that I would have loved you
with every smile within me

. . . even if you weren't
the most precious,
understanding, sweetest,
and most special sister
in the world.

— Carle Jordan

I'm So Thankful, Sister, that I Have You in My Life

You're not afraid to open up and show your
   thoughts and feelings to me.
You make me feel good about myself.
You're always there for me,
   and you'll let me be there for you.
I know I can turn to you whenever I need
   someone to understand me,
to hold me,
to reassure me when things go wrong.

When I look into your eyes,
I see all the caring that's inside you,
and knowing that you care about me
* somehow makes me feel safe.*

We have a rare communication between us
* that few people ever share,*
trusting each other enough to talk
* about our fears, our disappointments,*
and our dreams.
I feel so comfortable with you,
* so at home.*
I'm thankful that I have you
* in my life.*

— Sharon Leigh Johnson

Most of all, you're my sister . . .

You are my closest companion;
you are my best friend;
you are the person I most want
   to share the news with when
   things go right; and the one
   I rely on when things go wrong.
You are so many good things
   and so many qualities I love.

But most of all, you're my sister.
And you're something special to me
that no one else can ever be.

— Carey Martin

Sister, I Love to Recall Everything We've Shared Together

When we were younger,
  I never would have believed
that we would end up
  being best friends someday.
For years, we always seemed
  to be getting in each other's way
over and over again.
But as we got older,
and started to do more things together,
we discovered that we really
  could get along.
We began to share our thoughts,
dreams, and, finally, our fears.

We have built a trust
  between us,
a feeling of love and security
that will grow even more in
  the years to come.
Together, we laughed, we cried
  and got back on our feet,
over and over again.
I'm so glad that we have such
  an understanding relationship.
For having a sister like you
  for a best friend
means we'll never have to say good-bye.

— *Donna Marie Urban*

Thanks, Sister

Thank you for being so thoughtful
and for brightening my day.
Thank you for being someone
who always cares,
always takes the time
to do something nice.
Thank you for being
the kind of person
who can change an ordinary day
into something special!

— Deanna Beisser

Sister, You'll Always Be One of My Favorite People in the World

We've always been a little shy
about expressing our feelings
    for each other.
I don't tell you very often
    how much you mean to me,
and you don't often say it to me,
but I think we both know that
if you ever needed me
    or I ever needed you,
we'd be there for each other.

We may not live in the same
   house anymore,
but we're still close,
   and we always will be.
So I think it's time I told you
   something that I've been
   meaning to say
   for a long time . . .
I love you, and you'll always be
   one of my favorite people
   in this world.

— *Anna Marie Edwards*

Though Miles Separate Us, Sister, You Are Always Here in My Heart

It seems like only yesterday
that we were kids together,
and we had so much fun.
Now we live in different places, and
sometimes I find myself feeling
a little sentimental, happy,
and sad all at once.

I miss you and your smiles,
and I think about how very
special you are to me.
I know we are miles apart,
but that will never change the
feelings in my heart for you.

— Deanna Beisser

Our Closeness as Sisters Will Always Overcome Our Differences

Even though we've had our differences in the past, and things weren't always easy between us, deep down inside both of us we knew we loved each other, and we wanted each other to find happiness.

Sister, I guess it takes
growing up a little
and growing older
to realize how important
family is
and how much we really do care.
So for all the times
I've let go by
and for all the things
I didn't say
when I should have,
I want you to know now
that being sisters
isn't always easy,
but I wouldn't change it
for the world.
I really do love you.

— Laura Medley

Thinking of You, My Sister

I hope that it brings you a smile
to know how much
   you've been on my mind.

Every time I think of you,
I wish we lived closer together . . .
but I know
   in my heart
that we will always be
as near and as dear to each other
   as sisters and best friends
      can be.

— Collin McCarty

Always Sisters
and Forever Friends

We've always been friends . . .
and I know,
more than anything,
that we always will be.

But we're also sisters,
and because of that . . .
we share an understanding
that goes beyond
what two friends can share.
There are things I can tell you
that I can't say to anyone else . . .
and I think that you feel
the same way about me.
I am comforted
by that thought, and
by the knowledge that —
no matter what happens —

I'll always have you,
and you'll always have me,
to talk to, to confide in,
and to walk with
in every tomorrow.

That's real friendship.
That's understanding and
family love
and security and faith.

And that, to me . . .
is great.

— *Carey Martin*

To My Sister

Sister,
there are three simple wishes
that I hold in my heart
* for you.*
I wish for you
happiness and special times
for you to enjoy.
I wish for you good health
in everything you do.

But most of all,
I wish for you
the truest love there is
in the world,
and that is the love of family.
I know how much that means to you,
because it will always mean
* so much to me.*

— Deanna Beisser

Sister, You're in My Thoughts Every Day

I think about you
more than you know.
There are a lot of times,
day after day,
when something will
remind me of you
and the memories we share.
I laugh to myself about
our happy times,
and still feel a little sad
remembering our disappointments.
Life has certainly given us both
our fair share of changes,
but through it all,
we've known that, whatever happened,
we could depend on one another.

Sister,
there's rarely a day that goes by
when I don't think of you.
I feel thankful
that we are sisters;
I feel blessed
that we are family;
and I feel the love we share
that binds our lives together.

— Deanna Beisser

ACKNOWLEDGMENTS

We gratefully acknowledge the permission granted by the following authors to reprint their works.

Denise Vega-Perkins for "Being My Sister Makes You Different from Any Friend I've Ever Had." Copyright © Denise Vega-Perkins, 1989. All rights reserved. Reprinted by permission.

Debbie Avery Pirus for "Sister, I just wanted you to know. . . ." Copyright © Debbie Avery Pirus, 1989. All rights reserved. Reprinted by permission.

Carol Maatta Oberg for "With Love, from Sister to Sister." Copyright © Carol Maatta Oberg, 1989. All rights reserved. Reprinted by permission.

Jane Alice Fox for "Thanks, Sister, for the Times You've Shared with Me." Copyright © Jane Alice Fox, 1989. All rights reserved. Reprinted by permission.

Chris Ardis for "Sister, the Love We Have for Each Other Will Always Be a Part of Us." Copyright © Chris Ardis, 1989. All rights reserved. Reprinted by permission.

Donna Marie Urban for "Sister, I Love to Recall Everything We've Shared Together." Copyright © Donna Marie Urban , 1989. All rights reserved. Reprinted by permission.

A careful effort has been made to trace the ownership of poems used in this anthology in order to obtain permission to reprint copyrighted materials and to give proper credit to the copyright owners.

If any error or omission has occurred, it is completely inadvertent, and we would like to make corrections in future editions provided that written notification is made to the publisher: BLUE MOUNTAIN PRESS, INC., P.O. BOX 4549, Boulder, Colorado 80306.